D1164823

A Koala's World

written and illustrated by Caroline Arnold

PICTURE WINDOW BOOKS
Minneapolis, Minnesota

Special thanks to our advisers for their expertise:

Peter Courtney, Divisional Curator, Native Fauna
Melbourne Zoo, Parkville, Victoria, Australia

Susan Kesselring, M.A., Literacy Educator
Rosemount–Apple Valley–Eagan (Minnesota) School District

Editor: Christianne Jones
Designer: Hilary Wacholz
Page Production: Melissa Kes
Art Director: Nathan Gassman
The illustrations in this book were created with cut paper.

Picture Window Books
5115 Excelsior Boulevard
Suite 232
Minneapolis, MN 55416
877-845-8392
www.picturewindowbooks.com

Printed in the United States of America.

 All books published by Picture Window Books
are manufactured with paper containing at least
10 percent post-consumer waste.

Library of Congress Cataloging-in-Publication Data
Arnold, Caroline.
A koala's world / written and illustrated by Caroline Arnold.
p. cm. – (Caroline Arnold's animals)
Includes index.
ISBN-13: 978-1-4048-3984-7 (library binding)
1. Koala–Australia–Juvenile literature. 2. Parental behavior in
animals–Australia–Juvenile literature. I. Title.
QL737.M384A76 2008
599.2'5–dc22   2007032884

Koalas are divided into two main groups—northern and southern. This book is about Queensland koalas, which are part of the northern group.

Where they live: Australia

Habitat: coastal islands, tall eucalyptus forests, and low woodlands

Food: leaves, buds, and stems of eucalyptus trees

Length: 2 to 2.5 feet (65 to 75 centimeters)

Weight: 12 to 17.5 pounds (5.4 to 7.9 kilograms)

Animal class: mammal

Scientific name: *Phascolarctos cinereus*

Koalas are marsupials. A female marsupial has a special pouch where her baby is carried and fed. A baby koala is called a joey. Climb a eucalyptus tree and learn about a koala's world.

Trees provide koalas with food, shelter, and safety.

4

In an Australian forest, a koala climbs a tall tree. With a plump body and round ears, she looks like a living teddy bear. Strong limbs, sharp claws, and a fine sense of balance make her a good climber.

The koala picks a tender leaf to eat. When the koala is done eating, she finds a wide branch and sits down. She is getting ready to have a baby.

At birth, a baby koala is about
the size of a jelly bean.

The baby koala has just been born. Her eyes are closed, and she has no fur. The baby crawls along her mother's belly and into her warm pouch.

The baby will stay in the pouch for about seven months, growing bigger each day. Inside the pouch, she drinks her mother's milk.

meadow argus butterflies

As usual, the mother koala eats and sleeps while her baby is growing inside her pouch. She finds her favorite foods on eucalyptus, or gum, trees. She likes the tender leaves at the tips of the branches.

The mother koala is a fussy eater. She sniffs each leaf before eating. If the leaf does not smell right, she will try a different one.

An adult koala eats between 1 and 1.5 pounds (0.45 and 0.7 kg) of leaves, buds, and stems each day.

sulphur-crested cockatoos

The baby is now 7 months old. Her eyes are open, and her body is covered with soft gray fur.

The baby takes her first peek at the outside world. She looks up at her mother's furry face. She looks down and sees leafy branches. *Skwak! Skwak!* The baby hears a flock of noisy birds. In a week or so, she will be ready to explore.

At 7 months, a baby koala is about 8 inches (20 cm) long.

The baby is ready to come out of the pouch. At first, she stays close to her mother. But as she grows stronger, she practices climbing on her own. She hangs on with her claws and pulls herself up the tree. When she gets tired or thirsty, she crawls back into her mother's pouch.

Claws on the hands and feet help a koala climb. Ridged skin on the bottom of the feet grip the tree.

Now the young koala is 8 months old. She is too big to go into the pouch. Instead, she rides on her mother's back. The young koala can reach leaves by herself and find her own food.

dingoes

When the koalas run out of fresh leaves, they must look for a new tree. On the ground, the koalas watch and listen for danger.

Aroo! Aroo! They hear dingoes nearby. The mother and baby quickly climb the nearest tree.

The main pedators of koalas are foxes and dingoes, or wild dogs.

As the young koala grows, she spends more time on her own. But at nap time, she always sleeps with her mother. They find a sturdy branch and curl up into a ball.

The koalas eat and sleep both day and night. Their thick fur keeps them warm and dry, even when it is windy or rainy. When it is hot, the treetops are a good place to find a cool breeze.

Australian water dragon

Koalas are super sleepers. They nap 18 to 20 hours a day. They are active mainly at night and at the beginning and end of the day.

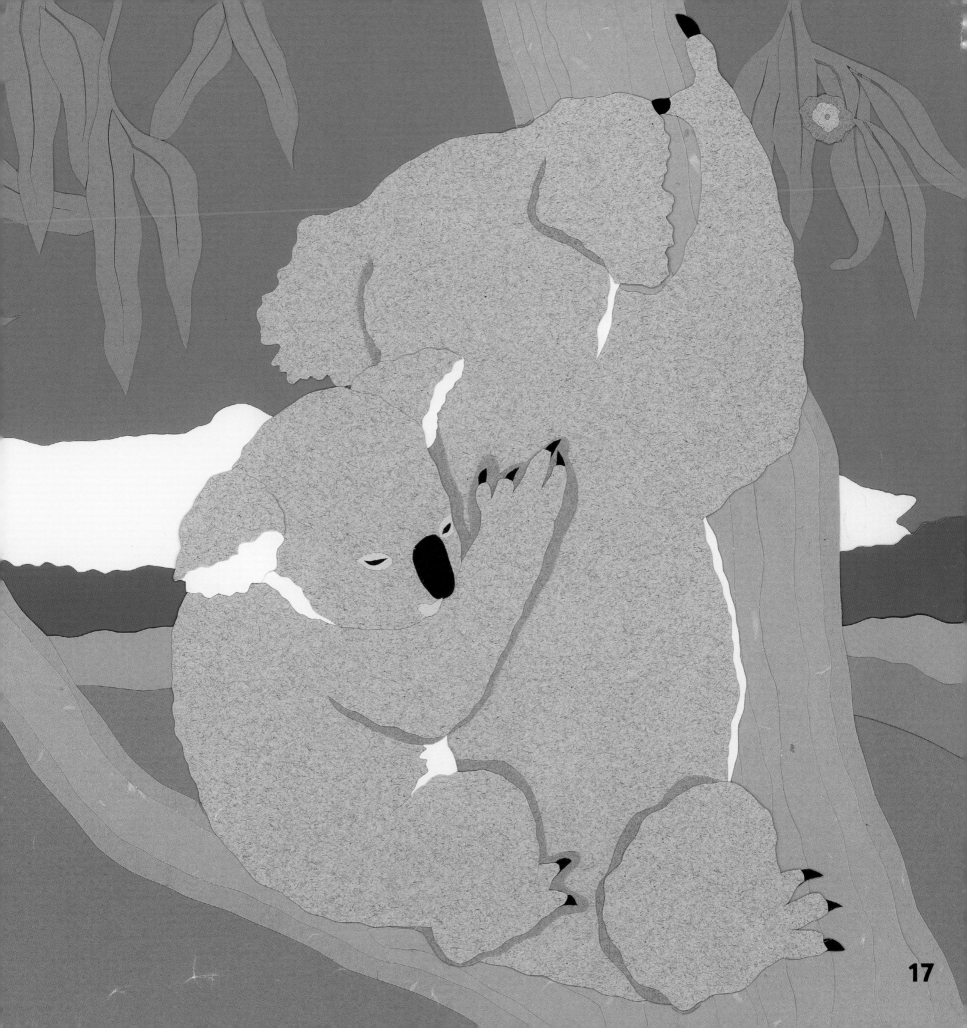

One male koala and two other females live nearby in the forest. Each koala has its own territory and its own trees. The young koala knows which trees are in her mother's territory. No other koala can eat from these trees. A male koala rubs his scent on the trees to mark his territory.

A male koala has a special scent gland on his chest. It produces smelly oil.

Now the young koala is 1 year old. She is big enough to be on her own. She will leave her mother and go to another part of the forest. She will find another group of koalas and her own trees. In another year, she will be ready to mate. Then she will become a mother, too.

Where do koalas live?

Koalas live in forests along the coasts of Australia. They are divided into two groups—northern koalas and southern koalas. Northern koalas are smaller and include the Queensland and northern New South Wales koalas. Southern koalas are larger and include koalas found in southern New South Wales, Victoria, and South Australia.

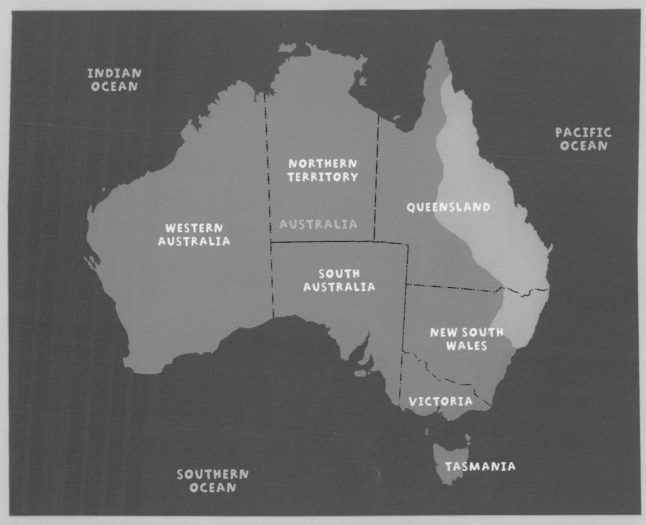

INDIAN
OCEAN

PACIFIC
OCEAN

NORTHERN
TERRITORY

QUEENSLAND

WESTERN
AUSTRALIA

AUSTRALIA

SOUTH
AUSTRALIA

NEW SOUTH
WALES

VICTORIA

SOUTHERN
OCEAN

TASMANIA

 **NORTHERN KOALAS**

 **SOUTHERN KOALAS**

Koala Fun Facts

Long Lives

Koalas in the wild may live from 10 to 15 years. In zoos, they live from 12 to 16 years.

Fussy Eaters

There are about 600 different kinds of eucalyptus trees in Australia, but koalas eat from fewer than 40 of them. Koalas must move from tree to tree to find enough food.

Poison Leaves

Eucalyptus leaves are poisonous to most animals. Koalas are one of the few animals that can eat them. Their digestive systems remove the poison from the leaves.

Sharp Teeth

A koala has two sharp teeth in the front of its mouth. They are good for tearing leaves or stripping bark. In the back of its mouth are five pairs of flat chewing teeth.

Rarely Drink

The native Australian word koala means "drinks no water." Eucalyptus leaves provide most of the water that koalas need.

Not a Bear

In 1816, when people gave the koala its scientific name, they made a mistake. The name means "furry, pouched, gray bear." But the koala is not a bear at all. It is more closely related to other marsupials such as wombats and possums.

Safe in the Pouch

A strong muscle keeps the pouch tightly closed when the baby koala is inside. The muscle relaxes when the baby is ready to come out.

Glossary

digest—*what an animal's body does to break down its food and take out what it needs to live and grow*

eucalyptus—*evergreen trees in the myrtle family; also known as gum trees*

habitat—*the place or natural condition in which a plant or animal lives*

joey—*a baby marsupial*

mammals—*warm-blooded animals that feed their babies milk*

marsupial—*animal whose babies are carried in a pouch on the mother's body*

predators—*animals that hunt and eat other animals*

To Learn More

More Books to Read

Hewett, Joan. *A Koala Joey Grows Up.* Minneapolis: Carolrhoda, 2004.

Lang, Aubrey. *Baby Koala.* Brighton, Mass.: Fitzhenry and Whiteside Limited, 2004.

Lee, Sandra. *Koala.* Chanhassen, Minn.: The Child's World, 2007.

On the Web

FactHound offers a safe, fun way to find Web sites related to topics in this book. All of the sites on FactHound have been researched by our staff.

1. Visit *www.facthound.com*

2. Type in this special code: 1404839844

3. Click on the FETCH IT button.

Your trusty FactHound will fetch the best sites for you!

Index

Look for all of the books in Caroline Arnold's Animals series:

A Kangaroo's World
A Killer Whale's World
A Koala's World
A Panda's World
A Penguin's World
A Platypus' World
A Wombat's World
A Zebra's World